# This coloring book belongs to:

..................................................
..................................................

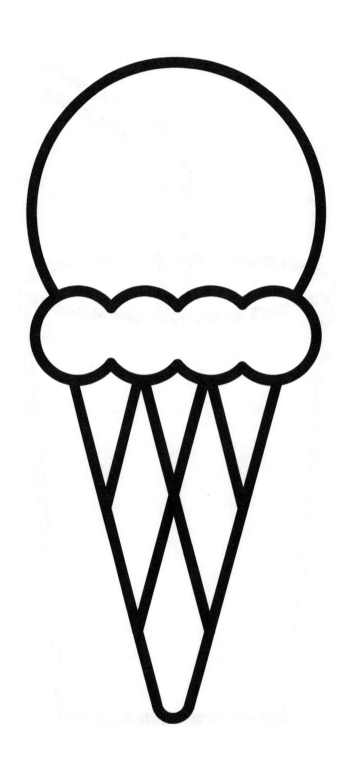

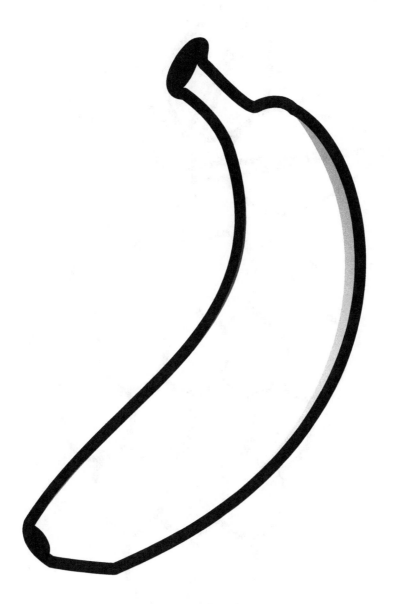

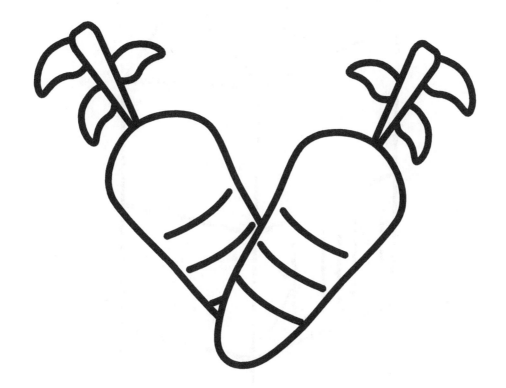

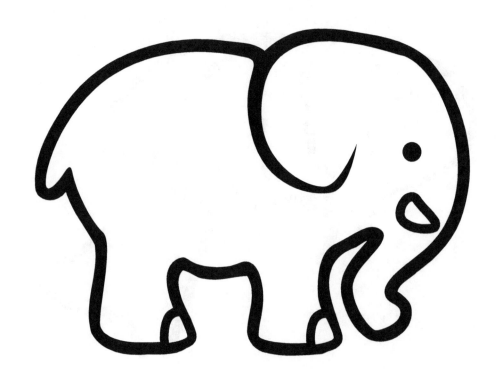

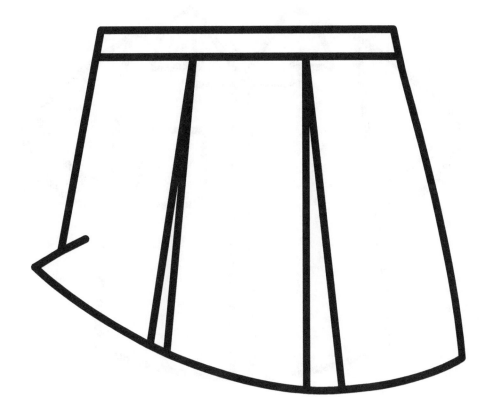

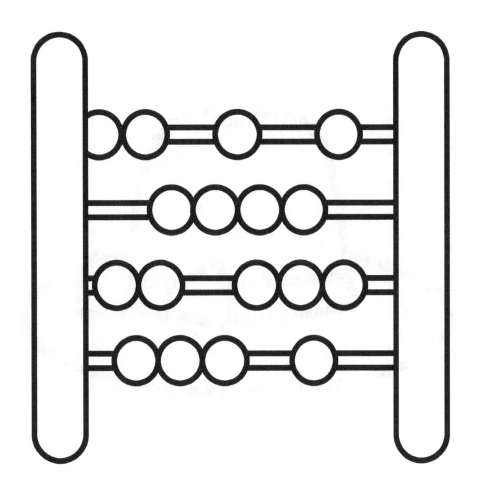

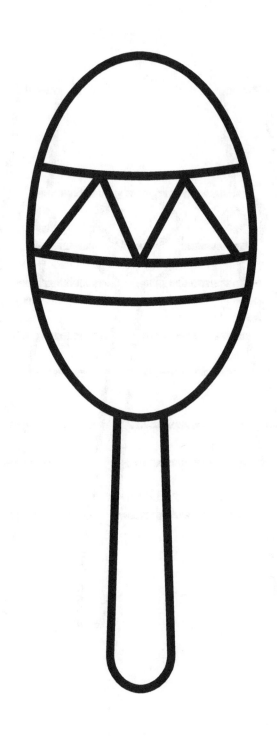

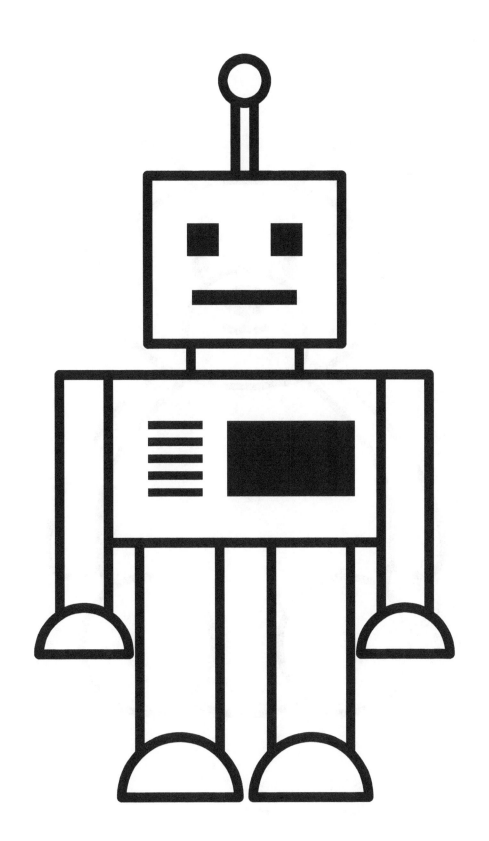

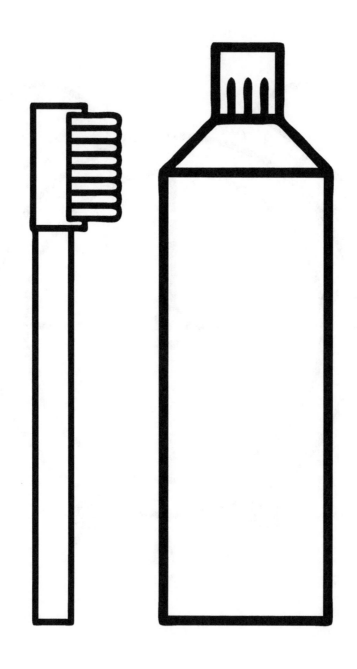

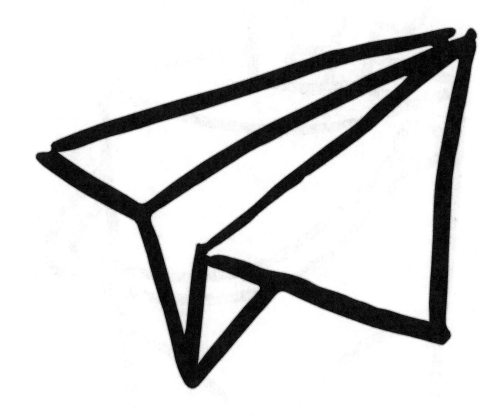

www.ingramcontent.com/pod-product-compliance
Lightning Source LLC
LaVergne TN
LVHW060705020325
804892LV00012B/384